P9-CBI-686

contemporary asian
KITCHENS AND
DINING ROOMS

Karina Zabihi and Chami Jotisalikorn
photos by Luca Invernizzi Tettoni

PERIPLUS

Published by Periplus Editions with
editorial offices at 130 Joo Seng Road
#06-01 Singapore 368357

Copyright © 2004 Periplus Editions
Photos © 2004 Luca Invernizzi Tettoni

ISBN 0 7946 0178 2
Printed in Singapore

Distributed by:
North America, Latin America and Europe
Tuttle Publishing, 364 Innovation Drive,
North Clarendon, VT 05759-9436, USA
tel (802) 773 8930; fax (802) 773 6993
email: info@tuttlepublishing.com
www.tuttlepublishing.com

Asia Pacific
Berkeley Books Pte Ltd, 130 Joo Seng Road
#06-01/03, Singapore 368357
tel (65) 6280 1330; fax (65) 6280 6290
email: inquiries@periplus.com.sg
www.periplus.com

Japan
Tuttle Publishing, Yaekari Building, 3F,
5-4-12 Osaki, Shinagawa-ku,
Tokyo 141-0032
tel (813) 5437 0171; fax (813) 5437 0755
email: tuttle-sales@gol.com

contemporary asian kitchens and dining rooms: culinary yin and yang

To quote American writer Arnold Lobel, "All's well that ends with a good meal." If the dining room is the heart of the home then the kitchen is the pulse that feeds it. Today's kitchens are finally making their own bold design statement: stylish, streamlined and full of character. Innovations in quality products and materials make the modern kitchen a functional yet visually stunning space. And, just as paintings and artwork contribute greatly to the harmony of a dining room, so the plethora of modern gadgets and utensils are introducing an artistic element to the workspace of the house. Few kitchens today would be complete without at least one modern designer accessory.

The concept of an open-plan kitchen and dining room is a relatively new one in Asia. Historically, the kitchen was seen as a no-frills, utilitarian place where maids and cooks rushed around preparing meals, and where little thought was given to the décor. It was a place to be hidden from view, away from the guests.

The 1950s saw a transformation in kitchen design in America, and Europe. Overnight, women whose apron strings had been securely tied to the kitchen sink had access to all the mod cons they could wish for and both food preparation and mealtimes underwent something of a revolution. The dream kitchen of the '50s had all a woman needed for an easy, streamlined lifestyle and as more women worked outside the home in America, the TV dinner gradually became the quick and convenient way to eat.

Not all cultures embraced this American dream. In the more traditional countries of southern Europe and in Asia, where an extended and strong family unit was the norm, mealtimes—and by default the kitchen and dining rooms—were still the core around which family life was focused.

In the past, many Asian homes featured two kitchens—the "working kitchen" often situated outside or behind the house where messy stir-frying was done and the "dry kitchen" where plates and utensils were kept and food was assembled before serving. This is sometimes still the case today.

Over the years, the kitchen has evolved from being just a functional adjunct to the main house to an entertainment center and showpiece. And where once Asian designers and architects were very much influenced by the West, many firms featured here, including aKTa-rchitects, HYLA and Eco-id, are now creating kitchen and dining spaces with a more Asian sensibility while exploiting western technological inventions.

Beginning in the 1980s, major innovations were introduced in restaurant design. Fusion cuisine and celebrity chefs—television's new heartthrobs—changed the way we thought about eating and cooking. Terence Conran helped revolutionize the modern restaurant with his cutting-edge "kitchens on view" such as those at Quaglino's and Mezzo in London while Ed Tuttle created a graceful and new Asian style at the Aman resorts. Increased global travel and changes in restaurant design naturally had a trickle-down effect on how domestic kitchens were designed.

More recently, Japanese designers like Super Potato's Takeshi Sujimoto and his protégé Yasuhiro Koichi have been instrumental in creating restaurants that are both the ultimate in contemporary design yet also reflect their eastern locale. Mezza9 in Singapore's Grand Hyatt, La Scala at the Sukothai in Bangkok and The Cliff at the Sentosa Resort and Spa in Singapore are just some examples of the groundbreaking new Japanese style of restaurants.

Changing trends in Asian cooking have also determined how kitchens are designed. Where once a gas stove would

have sufficed for wok cooking, more people are turning to "cleaner" options such as electric hobs and specially—and often aesthetically—designed gadgets including electric woks and rice cookers. This development has in turn affected the culture of dining and entertaining in Asia. As one Singaporean homeowner said, "when we first met with our architect to talk about the house that we wanted to build, one of the earliest and most exciting points of our discussion was about designing the kitchen, dining and living rooms as a contiguous space complete with a long table spanning the kitchen and dining area. Since cooking and entertaining feature quite prominently in our lives, and given that I'm always stuck in the kitchen when guests arrive, this would be a brilliant way for me to cook and entertain our guests at the same time without them having to come into the kitchen."

Freed from the conventional restrictions of four walls, the dining room is also becoming more experimental in layout and design. Asia's tropical climate has inspired many designers in Singapore, Bali and elsewhere to incorporate the outdoors with the indoors. Dining rooms seamlessly merge with gardens and pools providing avenues for balmy al fresco dining.

above Orbit Design gave this bachelor's dining room in Bangkok a slick and sexy look with metallic wall paint, stainless steel and glass.
above right The generous kitchen counter and roomy benches double as additional dining space during parties in this Bangkok loft.
right Accessories in fruit colors add whimsical charm to the white-on-white dreamscape of this minimalist kitchen counter in Thailand.
opposite An immense cascading wall of water frames this floating dining platform at The Cliff at the Sentosa Resort and Spa.

International design companies such as Boffi, Miele and Arclinea now pave the way for variation and experimentations in our kitchen designs—with the help of product designers and renowned architects like Antonio Citterio. New brands are increasingly available at Asian showrooms such as Kitchen Culture and Cream 136 in Singapore where customer demands for functionality, style and innovation are paramount.

With the wealth of design shops in the region, home-owners are spoilt for choice when it comes to decorating their homes. However, there is a growing trend for custom-made furniture specially designed for a space which also reflects the owners' individuality and personality. Many Asian homeware designers, like Pesamuan and Jenggala Keramik in Bali, have turned tableware into an art form with crockery and accessories that are imaginative and stylish. In keeping with the region's eclectic and diverse cultures, the emphasis in the design of kitchens and dining rooms is on tastefully blending eastern and western elements to create a "fusion" style.

In Bali, two artists have employed their distinctive and vibrant artwork to spectacular effect in their house (page 60). Modern calligraphy reiterates the theme of contemporary Asian in a bachelor apartment in Singapore (page 96) and in Malaysia, Indian antiques offer an interesting counterpoint to a thoroughly modern space (page 52).

above Vibrant reds provide a dramatic contrast to the biscuit and black palette in this al fresco dining area at The Club at The Legian. Mother-of-pearl inlay on the table introduces a delicate touch.
right Styling a table is all about experimentation and innovation. In this Singapore apartment, the table settings reflect the linear architecture while also introducing a modern Asian sensibility.

Innovations in materials are also liberating the design of kitchens. While limestone and ceramic tiles are still used for counter tops, many designers are exploring solid surface materials such as Corian for its sleek and satin finish, while durable stainless steel gives a modern and minimalist effect.

Asians are also experimenting with the shape of their dining tables. Whether it is round, square or oval, any shape and size goes as long as it enhances the space. And it is no longer *de rigueur* for the dining table and chairs to match. In one of the Singapore homes featured in this book, a boardroom office table is used to great effect as a spectacular dining table paired with contemporary leather chairs (page 33) while in Thailand, tree trunks were hollowed out to make benches offsetting the overall modern look of the dining room (page 34).

Asia has always been able to assimilate western innovations while adhering to its own traditions. Whether it is a shophouse kitchen in Singapore that is given an industrial makeover, or a house in Bangkok where the original servants quarters are converted into a stylish dining room, or a kitchen in a Balinese villa that is open to the elements, the dining rooms and kitchens shown in these pages are testament to the unparalleled variety of designs and styles in the region.

The houses and apartments featured in this book illustrate the enormous changes that have taken place in the design of kitchens and dining rooms. The contemporary Asian dining room and kitchen gracefully blends the functional with the stylish, and modern innovations with the oriental charm that ultimately defines the lifestyle we lead. Integration rather than isolation is the key.

left A condo kitchen in Bangkok's Sky Villas embodies the dramatic new attitude to the cooking space. The custom-designed kitchen counter has the high-gloss chic of a trendy Japanese restaurant, taking snacking to a style high.
below These intricately wrought chopsticks, crisp white napkins and silk ties artfully blend Asian tradition and contemporary style.

shades of sophistication   Conceived as a series of bungalows stacked vertically, the clean and restrained architectural style of these Singapore apartments designed by Calvin Sim of Eco-id Architects is reflected in the luxurious open-plan dining area.

above Rich fabrics and a muted color palette convey a sense of elegant, understated opulence appropriate for the well-traveled and sophisticated homeowner. Heavy drapes frame full-height glass windows and the abundant foliage beyond.

left A Fendi leather console table against Roselle Montclair fabric-paneled walls is a great showcase for this simple display.

opposite An inviting entertaining space is all about blending hues, textures and creating stunning table settings. The custom-made pendant by Lightcraft that runs almost the entire length of the dining table fills the compact space, making it appear larger than it is. The dark and subtle tones of the table setting complete the graceful look of the dining room.

play of light   The chocolate-and-vanilla interior at the Anantara Resort & Spa Hua Hin's Italian restaurant shows the magical effects of subtle lighting, as hidden light sources lend a glowing allure to the basic palette of wood and cream-colored walls.

above Recessed backlighting and the shimmer of glass create a romantic ambience at this table for two while multiple lanterns lend a sense of symmetry.
left Square shapes provide a modern alternative to the usual round plates, a theme echoed in the square vases, given an Asian accent with water lilies.
opposite Removable patterned runners on the armchairs allow the seats to be dressed up or down for different occasions.

an open plan Like many large houses in Thailand, the home of Rika Dila has two kitchens: a main cooking kitchen at the back of the house, and a western-style "dry kitchen" inside, used as a pantry and serving area for pre-cooked food and drinks.

above When the kitchen is in open view from the dining and living room areas, handsome kitchenware is called for. This Boffi cabinetry is fashionable as well as functional. The stainless steel designer juicers from Habitat keep the look stylish.

right The view from the living room shows that there is no division of space among the kitchen, dining and sitting areas. In this open-plan concept, all areas merge into one room, giving a simple ease to living and entertaining.
opposite The clean-cut look of the Minotti table and leather chairs makes the combination a versatile palette for any type of table setting. Behind the table is a painting of a womb by Thai artist Pinaree Sanpitak.

tropical zest   When Guz Wilkinson Architects redesigned this old shophouse in Singapore, the main objective was to "get as much light and nature into the heart of the house as possible" by incorporating natural materials against a white palette.

left The white floors and walls enhance the airy feel of the core of the house. Bright flowers and the earth-toned crockery add zest to the overall design. The pool, with its abundant foliage and "floating" stepping stones, connects the front and the rear sections of the house.

above The rear block of the house was a new addition. Seen here through full-height glass doors in the front living area, the space exhibits a modern style while still retaining the character of the old shophouse. Curved wooden chairs from Space reflect the tone of the wood used for the door handles.

humor and harmony
Clean, contemporary lines make Andy and Michele Wilkinson's kitchen in their Singapore condominium designed by K2LD Architects both a practical space for cooking and a great venue for entertaining friends.

left Michele has a self-confessed passion for cows and is an avid collector of all things bovine. Her witty collection includes tea pots, butter knives, place mats and egg cups from all over the world.
below left Artist Hollis Fingold makes household objects into animal art—such as this fun phone that Andy and Michele bought in Hong Kong.
below right A cow-inspired jug makes for an unusual container for kitchen utensils and a great talking point.
opposite The kitchen plays an important role in Andy and Michele's lives. They were very particular about what fittings they wanted, so Quality Renovations custom made everything according to their specifications. Stainless steel and white Corian make for a fresh and uncluttered look. The open-plan design means the couple are never isolated from their guests while entertaining. The edgy, minimalist bar stools are from Trax.

gracious living For a couple who entertain regularly, "it was essential that the kitchen was connected visually to the dining, and the dining to the living area," explains Benny Cheng of space_craft, who designed this large house in Singapore.

left The contrast of dark wood and white marble enhances the perfect symmetry of the dining area. This winning combination is echoed in the custom-made dining table and central bar console. The Fuscia 3 overhead lights by Achille Castiglioni from FLOS and a tranquil pool linking the dining and living room complete this model of harmony.

top Designed by Benny Cheng, this dark wood table with its marble centerpiece accentuates the overall concept of the space. An elegant and romantic dinner setting is created by playing with the theme of pure white and purple. The beaded napkin rings are from Barang Barang.

above The central bar fashioned from lush Bianca Calcutta Italian marble is the perfect spot for entertaining guests and creating cocktails. A cleverly designed sink doubles as a tray.

natural harmony   Located on a magical offshore island, The Cliff restaurant at
the Sentosa Resort and Spa in Singapore was designed by Japanese architect
Yasuhiro Koichi and offers the ultimate in sumptuous luxury and timeless elegance.

left Surrounded by sheer glass walls that double up as a wine cooler and display cabinet—a modern interpretation of *fin de siècle* opulence—this private chef's table offers an incredibly lavish and intimate dining experience. Translucent glass plates complement the muted tones of the leather "wicker" armchairs and wooden lattice base of the dining table.

above Yasuhiro Koichi's starting point for the restaurant's design was water. This private dining area sits on its own raised pavilion in a shallow pool, sheltered on one side by a stone wall of cascading water. The wall has a ridged texture which creates a shimmering ripple effect.

reflected splendor   Michele and Andy Wilkinson's dining room in their Singapore condominium designed by K2LD Architects proves that modern can also be romantic and sumptuous. It's all about subtle lighting and amazing attention to detail.

above Clever lighting installed under the table can be adjusted to enhance different moods. In the setting above, the emphasis is on a sensual display, high-lighted by these delicate wine glasses from Club 21.
left Red is forever rich and this dining service from Villeroy & Boch enhances the drama of the table setting.
opposite When it came to reno-vating their home, the owners wanted a space that delivered on the "wow" factor. A dark wood-paneled wall presents the perfect backdrop to this dining table fashioned according to the couple's specifications from onyx and stainless steel.

funky china   The Conrad Bangkok's Chinese restaurant, Eat Rice Drink Tea, has no access to the open air, so the design challenge was to distract the eye from the cave-like space with quirky décor that is at once modern, chic and distinctly oriental.

above This imaginative place mat is made from a real lotus leaf that has been treated and dyed, and the Chinese-style napkin ring, from green stones and a coin medallion. Each diner has his or her own teapot and cup.
left Velvet pillows adorned with *obi* belts made of Chinese silk add whimsical charm to the oriental theme.
opposite The windowless private dining room uses mirrors and lighting to create deeper dimensions. The round banquette is a contemporary touch that softens the room's rigid geometry.

white wisdom With a kitchen that serves as an inviting den and a dining room that is open on two sides to the garden, this house in Singapore designed by Sim Boon Yang of Eco-id Architects marries the best of eastern and western traditions.

above With glass doors that pull open to reveal the garden, dining becomes a real communion with nature.

right "The dinner service came from lots of places," says the owner. "Somehow it all fitted in!" Such eclecticism makes for a stunning table setting.

left An Ernesto Bedmar design, the marble dining table was originally used in the owner's boardroom. Here, paired with early Eames chairs, it makes an equally striking centerpiece.

opposite The long stone island that dominates the space is a great place for gathering and chatting. "When friends offer to cook for us—which is quite often—the kitchen becomes the dining room and living room as well," says the owner.

a house for dining The dining room in Arthur Napolitano's Bangkok residence is really a one-story building located behind the main house. Before Robin Lourvanij of Design Plus converted it, the room was used as a store room and servants' quarters.

above The generous skylight brings out the cheerful blue ceiling reminiscent of sky and sea. Benches fashioned from Balinese rice pounders made from hollowed-out tree trunks replace more formal chairs, enhancing the tropical island ease. The black and white on the cushion covers of traditional Balinese cloth symbolize good and evil.

right Sliding doors allow the dining room to open onto the lush garden and swimming pool, visible just beyond the Balinese-style fountain.

steely gaze   It's all about high-tech sophistication in this bachelor pad. Interior designers Orbit Design removed the original dividing walls and used stainless steel and a simple scheme of two colors for a minimal feel with maximum light and space.

above A extra wide counter top provides additional storage room while doubling as a generous serving counter for buffet entertaining. The white floor is made of crushed marble dust mixed with resin, which is easier to maintain than real marble.
left White pebbles in the floor recesses give additional texture to the white-on-white scheme.

The kitchen was entirely custom designed and made to fit the unconventional triangular space. Deceptively luxurious cabinets are made of medium density fiberboard (MDF) painted with a metallic dark blue paint that was chosen from car paint samples. Recessed metal handles and the stainless steel counter tops perfect the masculine look.

the art of living In this house in Singapore designed by Filipino architect
Michael Cu Fua, the dining room is both a paean to art and a reminder of the
old communal dining customs of the Philippines.

top Michael's sensual artwork lines the long corridor linking the living and dining rooms.
above This 150-year-old Kwan Yin head from a temple in Eastern China is one of the owner's most prized possessions.
left The wooden trestle table and benches Michael found in Dempsey Road seat 12 people and reflect traditional Filipino-style dining, where no one sits at the head of the table.

compact comfort In Bangkok's Siri Sathorn service apartment, designer Carolyn Corogin of C2 Studio managed to add dimension to a small space, while creating a masculine but comfortable style appealing to the mostly male executive clientele.

above The original kitchen walls were demolished, opening the narrow space and letting natural light into the kitchen. Cabinets in dark stained teak and black granite marble counter tops make for a serious executive look.

left Departing from traditional tile, the kitchen walls are lined with white laminated glass with a natural greenish tinge. This supports the design concept of creating a cool, clean interior in relief to the chaotic city outside. The wood flooring runs throughout the apartment and into the kitchen, giving the sense of a wide, flowing space.

opposite Dark stained wood and a white laminated glass table top continue the theme in the dining area. A mirrored column creates the illusion of greater depth. Air-conditioning vents and ceiling lights are hidden by a cove shelf which conceals the light source and bounces the light back onto the ceiling for a warm glow.

easy entertaining   As partners in the home décor firm, Paragon International, Bangkok homeowners Vichien Chansevikul and Michael Palmer found it only natural to design their own loft apartment, according to their specific entertaining style.

above Vichien and Michael love to entertain their guests with home-cooked meals. The loft apartment combines the kitchen, living and dining rooms in an open-plan space so that each area, while separate, is within easy view and access to the other parts of the room. In the kitchen, the open plan enables the homeowners and guests to cook and talk at the same time. The kitchen counter top doubles as a casual dining space where specially designed benches provide maximum seating for large buffet-style parties.

right The rooms are laid out around a square-shaped central atrium, so the owners chose the square as the core design motif, using a square grid pattern in various parts of the room. The round kitchen sinks offer visual contrast to the square blocks of frosted glass, which allow for optimum lighting with opaque privacy from the neighboring buildings in the vicinity.
opposite The triangular kitchen island was built for easy movement during cooking. Adding texture to the stark white color scheme, the custom-made wine cabinet accentuates the square theme echoed in the kitchen cabinet's frosted doors.

The unusual five-meter height of the loft apartment adds grandeur to the space. Framed by white diaphanous curtains, the dining area becomes a romantic stage for a meal. The leather-covered plant stands by Paragon Leather and the white leather chairs lend pristine elegance to the scene. An outdoor atrium beckons beyond the curtains, where a table by Thai furniture designer Ekarat Wongcharit takes pride of place. The curved metal table legs were inspired by the *chor fa* or roof gables of a traditional Thai house.

less is more Empty space can make the best décor element, as it frees the eye to appreciate the architectural features. In this Bangkok home, IA49 raised the ceiling to the roof, adding space, height and visual texture to the extremely long dining area.

left A pitted surface imparts a sense of character to the dining table, made of old wood that has been reworked into a more contemporary style. The table top is made of mango wood; the legs are made of teak. Paired with German chairs covered in faux suede, the effect is tropical and modern at the same time. **right** A glass corner overlooking the garden opens the space further outward. The white bench adds balance to the structural pillar while offering streamlined, spacious seating. The reclining nude is the work of Balinese-based American painter Symon.

space for thought   Nature is nurtured in this Singapore house designed by Sim Boon Yang of Eco-id Architects. The wall-to-wall window creates a perfect frame for the dining and kitchen space that marries both function and form.

above In designing the house, one of the most exciting discussion points with the architect was the creation of "a contiguous open space complete with a long table spanning the kitchen and dining area," says the owner. Clean and fuss-free, this is "a space that is not only nice to look at but very functional and a superb working kitchen."

right Beautiful accessories from The Link offer the ultimate in modern Asian table settings.

left The custom-made cement screed dining-cum-work surface paired with chairs from Limited Edition takes pride of place in the dining area and is enhanced by the soft tones of the limestone floor.

a rough diamond Combining industrial elements with the warmth of traditional furniture, Marcel Heijnen of Chemistry Design has created a second living space in his Singapore house that is at once both practical and inviting.

left The stainless steel cabinets, designed by Marcel, were made by a contractor who normally works on hawker centers.
below left Stripped of plaster, the kitchen wall "takes pride in its imperfections," says Marcel. The exposed brick brings out the cool sheen of the glasses and complements the earthy tones of the ceramic collection.
below right Neat hanging racks filled with an assortment of stainless steel cutlery add to the industrial feel of the kitchen.
opposite The rugged appeal of the kitchen is created by pairing bare brick walls with a dark-tinted cement floor and iconic, old-fashioned Southeast Asian "coffee shop" table and chairs with a traditional Chinese cabinet.

seductively simple Playing with different textures and floor levels, the dining room of this house in Kuala Lumpur, designed by Ernesto Bedmar of Bedmar & Shi, exemplifies tropical living while the Indian antiques add a distinctive edge.

left Surrounded by nature and filled with light, the dining room is "aesthetically the most beautiful space in the house," say the owners. Flanked on two sides by water, the dining room seems to be floating. Above the dining table hangs an unusual pendant carved according to Indian feng shui. The nine squares represent the nine planets of the Indian zodiac. Other unusual touches—such as the antique pillar used as a banister—give this house oodles of character and charm.

above Water, an element used to suggest peace and tranquility, also plays an important role in the design. The wall of black Malaysian granite provides a stunning backdrop to the room and complements the colors of the dining table and chairs from Moie. A low window cut into the wall offers stunning views of the courtyard—"the outside never actually leaves you," say the owners of the house.

upbeat downtown   "A striking living standard for short stays matching the expectations of a demanding jet-set clientele," is how architect Fredo Taffin describes the hip Downtown Apartments he designed in Bali.

above This small but compact kitchenette has that modern "diner" feel about it. *Merbau* wood given a glossy white coat and the painted glass splashback make this a bright and airy niche, perfect for leisurely breakfasts.
left Tightly bunched red roses provide a dramatic punctuation to the wood and marble console.
opposite Modern art by Bali-based French artist Veronique Aonzo balances the furniture's clean, classic lines. Square napkin rings from Modula and funky flower vases add flamboyance.

thai take-out This formal dining room in a Bangkok penthouse is designed in the style of a traditional Thai house, but raw, thick-grained wood paneling paired with contemporary lighting give the classic motif a sophisticated modern edge.

The smooth, dark wood of the table and chairs gives a simple but solemn feel to the dining room, while the ceramic tableware in various tones of black renders the look au courant. An east–west mix of Murano glass vases and Asian ceramics is displayed in the cabinets.

functional flair When designing this spacious and open-plan kitchen in a large house in Singapore, the aim of K2LD Architects was to "try to look at it as a room with furniture rather than as a kitchen."

above With a nod to Scandinavian design, these flush floor-to-ceiling cabinets finished in a wood-grain post-formed laminate from Formwell, illustrate how storage units can augment a stylish kitchen. The interplay of horizontal and vertical handles, display niche and frosted glass-fronted cabinet provide chic detailing.

right The architects proposed an "open-plan design that would interact with the breakfast area and face the internal patio." White Corian counter tops, Crestial taps from Germany and a stainless steel splashback help to lift the asceticism of the room. Bright orange and acrylic accessories from Cream add a dash of color.

the art of color
Inspired by the architecture of Mies van der Rohe and Luis Barragan, artists Philip Lakeman and Graham Oldroyd's kitchen and dining area in their house in Bali can be described as "Mies meets Luis and goes *troppo*."

left Philip and Graham's home has the minimum of walls, thus allowing the interior and exterior spaces to merge into one. "We didn't want to separate the living area from the dining and kitchen space, but have one space where all the functional areas flowed into the other," they say. Brilliant blue tiles form a stunning back-drop in the generous kitchen where a stainless steel bench doubles as a serving counter.

top left This collection of simple yet alluring ceramics was made in Pesamuan, a company owned by the duo.
top right Bottles fashioned from recycled materials show the artists' ingenuity.
above This yellow-and-blue crockery set is a example of Philip and Graham's use of strong colors as an essential element in their work.
above right Anthuriums offset by a simple vase add a masculine touch to the quixotic space.

left Philip and Graham have been economical with the amount of furniture and objects included in their space. "We love all our interior items and therefore allow them to stand proud within the interior," as witnessed by this large circular dining table inlaid with tiles from Pesamuan. The blank wall provides an ideal backdrop for displaying their dramatic artwork.

top Ceramic earth-toned plates and bowls made by the artists reflect the simplicity of design that Philip and Graham both admire and also add character to the table setting.

above "We believe that color and its application can create various different environments and moods," say Graham and Philip. The combination of the silk napkins and matching place mats paired with celadon crockery pick up the colors of both the artwork and foliage outside.

free flow A luxury of space is embodied in this Bangkok dining room with its panoramic views. Sliding glass walls replace the traditional barriers between indoors and outdoors, allowing the dining and living rooms and front courtyard to merge.

above The dining room opens into the front foyer and is thus accessible from the kitchen. A hand-blown glass bowl by Seiki Torige makes a stunning center-piece on the table of dark wood.
left Scandinavian flatware from Georg Jensen and lead crystal glasses add contemporary luxe.
opposite A Fendi leather console anchors the alcove at the far end of the room and offers a modern twist to the conventional wooden dining room sideboards. Hanging in the alcove is a painting by con-temporary Chinese artist Chen Yu, acquired from Lotus Lifestyle Gallery in Bangkok.

the charisma of crimson   At The Club at The Legian located in Bali's fashionable Seminyak district, designed by architect Shinta Siregar and interior designer Jaya Ibrahim, the traditional *balé* is given a striking modern makeover.

above Mother-of-pearl inlay—a delicate choice for these outdoor dining tables—is enhanced by the stylish combination of colors for the banquettes.

left The allure of this modern outdoor dining area lies in the interplay of shapes, textures and colors. The tone of the unusual black lacquer plates is brought out by the red and black napkins.

below left The combination of black and red is seductive. These cushions provide the invitation to sit back and enjoy the balmy tropical night.

opposite An integral part of any outdoor area in Bali, this *balé* is given a very contemporary rendition by the palette of rich colors, and is ideal for lounging and dining in true tropical al fresco style.

glass aerie   Designed by the owner with contemporary minimalism in mind, a glass-themed duplex penthouse rising high above the busy cacophony of Bangkok's streets offers a serene, sophisticated retreat in the clouds.

above The funky chromium chandelier from Stelline, the red dining chairs from B&B Italia and the Luna Piena wall lamp by Catelonni & Smith energize the monochrome interior while the hand-blown glass stupa by Seiki Torige balances the staircase.
left Lamont Contemporary specializes in giving classic motifs a modern look. These bowls have a shape associated with Thai craftwork, but are re-interpreted in beaten metal while the bronze vases resemble the curls of hair on Thai Buddha sculptures.
opposite The glass staircase was designed by the homeowner and made by local craftsmen. It separates the living and dining areas, and leads to a sitting room.

the best things in life   Modern is not often equated with sumptuousness but
the dining area of this hill-top apartment in Singapore designed by Sim Boon Yang
of Eco-id Architects oozes seductive sensuality.

left A triptych of paintings by renowned Cuban artist Enrique Martinez Celaya enhances the mood of the open-plan space. A 14-seater *chengai* wood and stainless steel dining table and leather chairs transcend modernity. Rather than removing the original marble on the floors, the architect ground out the shine to make it less "spic-and-span."

top Polished granite on the bar top frames the owners' original black-and-white photographs on the wall behind, and separates the dining and kitchen areas. The wall-to-wall hidden cabinets offer ample storage space.

above The pared-down elegance of the dining room is mirrored in the table settings. Coffee-cup holders from The Touch are used as miniature vases while cinnamon sticks add a quirky touch as rests for these chopsticks from Club 21. Geometric white plates introduce a zen quality.

blue moods Graham Oldroyd and Philip Lakeman's garden in their home in Bali "has many levels and secret areas." Here the lush foliage provides an enchanting fairytale setting for the outdoor dining space.

above Playing with shades from the deepest blue to the lightest turquoise for the table and banquettes and in the stacks of crockery designed by the artists is just the thing for this idyllic picnic venue.
right A blue stone flower and zany loungers are testaments to Philip and Graham's sense of fun when it comes to design.
opposite The pairing of blue and turquoise adds a whimsical and wistful charm to the setting and is an inspired choice for this outdoor dining table.

perfectly simple The overall concept for the dining and living areas in this house in Singapore designed by Han Loke Kwang of HYLA Architects revolves around an open space functioning as the center of all activities and "the heart of the house."

left The openness of this dining area is enhanced by the floating staircase made from a mild steel structure with *balau* timber strips. Indoor pools are now becoming increasingly popular in Asian homes, but eschewing the usual choice of fish and tropical plants, the architect opted for a mirror-still pool beneath the staircase, echoing the minimal elegance of the overall design. Bumble-bee yellow cups and saucers from Galerie Cho Lon give a playful touch to the Lola chairs and Artelano dining table.
opposite For the architect, "light and ventilation" were the main considerations when designing the kitchen. Working with Design Centro, HYLA has come up with a space that is both streamlined and spacious.

fusion mood   East–west chic is the style embodied in the private dining rooms at The Metropolitan Bangkok's Cyan restaurant. European and Asian furnishings combine, balancing the classic and contemporary against a minimal white palette.

left The severe contrast between deep black and bright white is softened by the sexy curvilinear lines and creamy smoothness of the molded chairs and rubber place mats. The chairs were custom designed for the hotel by Alberto Haberli and made in Italy. **below** The lightest of hand-blown Murano glass lamps is paired with a spartan Chinese classic cabinet to stunning effect. **opposite** When the focus is on empty space in a minimalist-style room, lighting becomes of first importance in changing the moods and dimensions of the space. By day, full-length glass walls (not shown here) let in maximum sunlight which floods the space, creating an airy openness. Come night, recessed downlighting lends an illusion of height to the ceiling while the dimmer control on the Murano glass lamps allows the owner to vary the mood from dramatic brightness to mellow softness.

shipshape chic   Small can indeed be beautiful as evidenced by this kitchen and
dining area of a duplex HDB apartment in Singapore designed by Raymond Seow
of Free Space Intent for a young nuclear family.

left The clean lines of this white
dining table and chairs from
V. Hive work well in this small
space, which measures 3.2 by
3.5 meters.
below left The celadon crockery
and arrangements of asparagus
and parsley are mirrored in the
green glass table top.
below right This simple towel
holder from Lifestorey makes its
own minimalist statement.
opposite Under-counter lighting
lifts the space in the kitchen. A
"solid surface" counter top, glass
splashback and aluminum finish
echo the color scheme of green,
white and grays.

let there be light   When Serene and Lars Sorensen asked Richard Ho and his architectural team to design their home in Singapore, the overall concept for the dining room was defined by a "simplicity that exudes warmth and coziness."

left The variegated colors of the Thai crockery enhance the natural tones of the solid teak dining table.
below The soft contours of Marc Newson's Wooden Chair for Cappellini harmonize with the natural surroundings of the garden just beyond the windows.
opposite "I like that minimalist feel with no fuss at all, straight lines and no upholstery," says Serene of the dining table and chairs she had custom made locally. Danish Le Klint lights above the table add to the airy feel of the room.

dining as art Seamlessly blending modern design with antique Asian elements, the dining room and kitchen of this detached house in Singapore designed by Italian architectural team Sottsass Associati proves that east does indeed meet west.

above A central free-standing work island from Gaggenau enhances the spaciousness of the kitchen. The custom-made table brings an added dimension to the room and is an inviting spot for light meals.
left Complementing the pair of Indonesian-Chinese scrolls in this dining room is the custom-made, glass-topped dining table teamed with chairs from Limited Edition. The unusual crockery from Jenggala Keramik adds a quirky touch.

bali bewitched With its enormous gallery-like spaces and sumptuous use of textures and finishings, Villa Ylang Ylang in Bali, owned by art historian Danielle and her businessman husband Mike Mahon, is reminiscent of a modern palace.

above A wrought-iron "candle tree" adds a touch of modern Gothic to the dining area.
right Gold underplates from India add a regal note and highlight the black dinner service from Jenggala Keramik. Delicate clusters of frangipani provide the Balinese element.
opposite Terrazzo speckled with mother-of-pearl on the floors imparts an elegant balance to the space. The three-meter, solid teak dining table is a collector's item. Paired with chairs designed by Danielle's company, Chair & Tango, and covered in Valentino fabric, it makes an impressive statement. Two diaphanous glass sculptures by Seiki Torige lend the finishing touch.

Unspoilt views of the ocean, a long, black sandy beach and harmony with the surroundings are undoubtedly some of the major attractions of Villa Ylang Ylang. The lawn provides a perfect setting for Danielle and Mike's collection of stone sculptures from Yogjakarta. The sumptuousness of the villa's interiors is mirrored here in the rich silks used on the chairs and adorning the *balé*. A sleek silver tea service from India, zany striped spoons and creative crockery from Jenggala Keramik place this outdoors dining area firmly in the modern context.

circular symmetry Part of the charm of the outdoor kitchen at Surga Villas in Bali, designed by architect Valentina Audrito, lies in the rounded contours and pastel tones that introduce a Mediterranean aspect to the design.

left With the accent on white, a custom-made wicker basket adds a rustic touch and is an eye-catching storage solution.
below Stacks of white and blue crockery from Jenggala Keramik offer a pleasing visual symmetry and echo the color scheme of the cushions in the informal living room above the kitchen.
opposite The combination of yellow and brilliant turquoise in this split-level kitchen makes for an interesting departure from the traditional Balinese style. The picture window integrates the garden into the kitchen, bringing in another design element to the space.

silk wrap Warm tones and shimmery surfaces transform a windowless alcove into a cozy, luxurious niche at the Conrad Bangkok's Chinese restaurant, Eat Rice Drink Tea, with blank silk walls and upholstery providing a subtle background sheen.

above Country-style ceramic ware in classic Asian earthy tones take on a contemporary twist when paired with funky metal pretzel chopstick holders. The napkin ring is made from elasticized Chinese beads.

above left Khun Suratsawadee Suksaidee of Flying Elephant Art & Handicraft Design sourced and custom designed the modern Chinese accessories. Metal bud vases resembling the smooth, sexy shapes of volcanic rock give a zen-like, distinctly Asian accent.

left The oriental theme is pulled together by layering accessories —such as a Chinese medallion carved from green stone, used as a napkin ring, as well as a hand-painted calligraphy runner.

opposite A small banquette and formal Chinese chairs lend this corner a sense of intimacy that is enhanced by lush silk walls, cushions and upholstery. In line with the Chinese custom of pairing items for balance, two lamps and a pair of Chinese vases flank this dining set.

a sanctuary of style   Shade and light, natural tones and the sculptural form of a
concrete honeycombed wall add an understated chic to the Faces restaurant at the
Bale in Nusa Dua in Bali, designed by Antony Liu and Ferry Ridwan.

above Echoing the linearity of the dining room design, black square plates from Jenggala Keramik offer a striking contrast to crisp white linen.

left The beauty of this open-air dining area lies in the straight lines and the contrasts of textures—cool stone, stainless steel and rattan chairs. The architects wanted a space that was "light and fun and communicated with the main pool area, the terrace and the open kitchen." The high ceilings present a very modern take on the traditional outdoor dining area.

white by design   The owners of Villa Uma de Begi in Bali wanted a kitchen that was not only "aesthetically pleasing," but echoed the "essentially traditional Balinese" villa concept and encouraged guests to participate in the culinary process.

right "We wanted guests to feel as if they were in Bali rather than in a kitchen that could be anywhere else in the world," says the owner. Hence the use of natural materials such as teak for the substantial central table, terrazzo for the flooring and a selection of white crockery. An overhead stainless steel light with fabric-wrapped cord makes for an interesting "ethnic chic" lighting concept.
left The kitchen is an integral part of the villa and the owners liked the interaction of the clean white lines with rich natural wood. The unusual shape of a traditional Indonesian cabinet makes for a pleasing counter-point to the wall-to-wall open shelves boasting an array of crockery from Jenggala Keramik.

bachelor bliss Double-height ceilings and a generous open-plan space in Mike
Tyldesley's Singapore apartment offered kzdesigns optimum opportunity to create
"a contemporary Asian space befitting a young, single man who loves to entertain."

left The dark tones of this custom-made dining table impart masculinity to the space while white accessories are in keeping with the contemporary Asian look that Mike and the designer were after. The custom-made honeycombed wine rack from Colonial Antique houses Mike's collection of fine wines. A Chairman Mao table runner from The Life Shop adds an idiosyncratic touch to the dining table. **opposite** A triptych of modern calligraphy on the wall created by Evershine Gallery provides the perfect backdrop to the 10–12-seater double dining tables. The combination of bamboo in one corner and stainless steel nightlight holders from The Touch Gallery above the day bed artfully blends the oriental with the modern. The specially designed acrylic and PVC standard lamps by kzdesigns cast a cool white glow to the room.

artful living Art mirrors art in the dining room of this spacious apartment in Singapore created by kzdesigns. "I wanted the vibrant modern art to animate the classical lines of the table," says the designer.

left "I like to confound people's expectations," the designer says, "by bringing unexpected elements into play." Here, classical dining is given a modern and romantic twist. The Wedgwood dinner service and French cutlery from d'apres nous contrast well with the mix of glassware and the eclectic choice of jugs as vases. Red bell peppers used as name card holders and amber roses make for a charming yet vivacious dinner setting.

opposite The dining room blends minimalist design with classical furniture. Unframed canvases by the Singapore-based British artist Loop give a contemporary edge to the elegant lines of the De La Espada walnut dining chairs and table with leather base. The crimson in one painting and chocolate tones of the other echo the color scheme of the room as a whole. The designer says, "The room is very large and I wanted to allow it the space to breathe instead of filling it with too many objects."

yin and yang attractions   When it came to the footprint of the kitchen, the owners of this detached house in Singapore designed by Kevin Tan of aKTa-rchitects were looking for a "large and clean-looking" place.

above The vintage, sepia-toned photographs counterbalance the modern wicker boxes from Club 21, which are ideal for storing kitchen knick knacks and also make for an attractive center-piece on this dark wood unit.
left What the owner loves most about this kitchen is that it is "spacious and convenient." The orange shades of the table and chairs from Italy make a bold statement in the otherwise pristine design of the Arclinea white units and black granite floor. The funky gadgets such as the Alessi jug and juicer from X•TRA make an interesting foil to the owner's Sung Dynasty set of plates.

The design of this spacious and airy dining room epitomizes the "modern tropical" look that the owners wanted. With windows that open the full length of the walls and simple yet stunningly designed railings by Kevin Tan, nature is very much part of the dining experience. The limestone floor lends a modern feel to the space while the inlaid ceiling provides a warm tone. Two Ming Dynasty pots balance the 10-seater dark wood table from the American Fine Furnishing Gallery and leather chairs from Space.

ethnic minimalism   This apartment in Singapore, designed by Geraldine Archer of
Mara Miri, seamlessly blends oriental antiques with clean, simple lines to create the
contemporary Asian feel desired by the clients, a young professional couple.

left The graceful lines of these champagne flutes from The Link hark back to the Art Deco period and accentuate the antique–modern dichotomy of the space. **below** The dark glass of the dining table demands a simple and elegant décor. The western and oriental settings from The Link are minimalist in their design yet opulent in style. **opposite** The smooth concrete blocks used in the floor, the glass top and the "open" design of the dining table and chairs accentuate the feeling of space in the small but inviting dining area. Pure silk blinds add texture to the space but "do not interfere with the clean lines of the wall nor invade the space with 'fullness'," says Geraldine. A clever niche set into the wall and birdcage lamp provide pockets of light. Red-black roses from Fluv enhance the romantic setting.

artful understatement "Intimate, cozy and restful" is how the owners of this large detached house in Singapore, designed by Kevin Tan of aKTa-rchitects, describe their sleek and stylish dining room.

above Custom-made furniture is a growing trend amongst home-owners who seek that individual touch. This solid wood table and chairs covered with Linea Tre fabric echo the muted neutral tones the owners sought in the dining room. Accessories from d'apres nous—such as the table runners used as place mats and delicate cutlery and glasses—offset the heavy wrought-iron candle holders.

right The owners love the muted, neutral colors employed in the dining room and in their art-work. When the sliding doors leading from the hall are closed, the space becomes an intimate sanctuary. The introduction of Asian artefacts softens the aus-tere linearity of the architecture.

left Contemporary art pieces by Andrew Wellman, the Bali-based Australian artist, and candle holders from Orientation nicely balance the cabinet's classic lines.

the art of kitchen culture The sheer size of the kitchen in this Singapore house designed by Kevin Tan of aKTa-rchitects and its wall-to-wall windows render it a to-die-for space. "I love big kitchens where everyone can hang out," says the owner.

above This streamlined unit from Arclinea is the perfect place to show off a triptych of glass vases filled with spices and the stainless steel mixer from Kitchen Aid.

left Modern accessories for a modern kitchen. This unusual pepper mill and olive oil jug bought on a trip to London accentuate the clean lines of the space.

opposite The owner wanted an enormous kitchen where she could "hang out and bake whilst someone else is doing the cooking." The contrast between the stainless steel central island, the cherry wood and the white of the Arclinea units adds oodles of character to this ultra-modern cooking den.

natural textures   The spotlight is on natural materials and textures in the Il Cielo
restaurant at the Dusit Thani Bangkok, where the design firm P49 focused on wood
and stone to achieve a country casual look chic enough for urban business dining.

above Glossy dark woods and shiny black leather signal corporate sophistication.
left Recessed shelving creates a gallery space to display a quirky herd of metal cattle crafted from a set of chopping knives. Ribbed stone walls, echoed in the wooden paneling, show the importance of texture in the design, with the focus on natural materials. The dining room opens onto an outdoor water feature and a fountain made of glass.

above Brilliant red bottles cele-
brate the room's drinking theme
while disguising the fact that the
room is windowless. This dining
niche has a low-slung sofa and
plump chairs that welcome diners
for intimate meals and to lounge
around for after-dinner drinks.
left Both functional and fashionable, this wine cellar and private
room in Il Cielo was designed
on an expansive scale, with a
capacious round table for generous corporate entertaining. The
wooden tabletop pattern echoes
the wood-paneled walls.
right Dramatic under-lighting
gives a vibrant radiance to these
bottles from Italy, designed by
Giovanni Bellini.

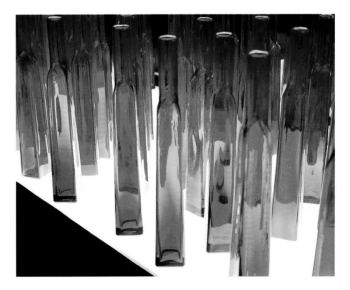

compact duo   Limited spaces in urban highrises don't always mean a sacrifice of style. A combined kitchen and dining area in this condo unit in Bangkok's State Tower shows how a small space can embody style with clean-cut lines and a basic palette.

above A small kitchen island defines the kitchen area while serving multiple functions as sink, storage and cooking work space. The addition of a stool turns it into a breakfast nook.

right This corner is part of the living room and kitchen, but a rug and a wall ledge define the area as a separate dining room. A basic black-and-white palette carried through in the minimal lines of an Asian dining set keeps the look streamlined and elegant, while contemporary paintings by American artists Tracy Hamer (right) and Symon (left) keep the mood fresh. Both artists are currently based in Bali.

weekend white   High ceilings and an all-white interior evoke high spirits and a
lighthearted mood in the kitchen and dining area of this weekend home in Thailand
designed by Robert Boughey & Associates.

above This stylish round basin of beaten metal and the elegant faucet are fashionable fixtures in place of the standard-issue stainless steel sink.

above left Exuberant plastic kitchenware keeps the mood festive for casual weekend dining.

left A play of textures adds dimensions to the white-on-white scheme. A plastic chair sits under a mixed media work by Thai artist Tawul Praman depicting a monk's fan. The white plastic waste bin has a zippered side detail.

opposite A spray of delicate purple blossoms appears to float in mid-air like an ethereal vision when displayed in a horizontal glass vase placed on a glass-topped dining table. The dining and kitchen area is generously proportioned for entertaining weekend guests. The counter is used as a "dry kitchen" and pantry for entertaining purposes, while the real cooking takes place in the "wet kitchen" at the back of the house.

honeyed overtones   Through the use of burnished amber and rich chocolate tones combined with the warmth of wood, Index Design has created an intimate and elegantly modern apartment at the Equatorial in Singapore.

above The three unusual acrylic panels created by Index Design—with minute perforations which allow for the placing of delicate flowers—introduce a quirky element in one corner of the dining area. The mirror completes the wood-paneled wall and brings an added dimension into the space, while the custom-made dark wood dining table adds to the aura of effortless elegance.
left The approach to this apartment was to "define a space without compromising its visual impact," says Angelena Chan of Index Design. "This was achieved via the introduction of the teak timber feature wall and screen." The wall provides a warm focal point while the slat screen acts as a divider between the living and dining areas. A FLOS light provides the one bright accessory in this overall honey-toned dining room.

organic architecture Surrounded by paddy fields in Bali's Kerobokan district, this villa designed by GM Architects incorporates the natural environment through the use of organic building materials while adhering to the best of modernist architecture.

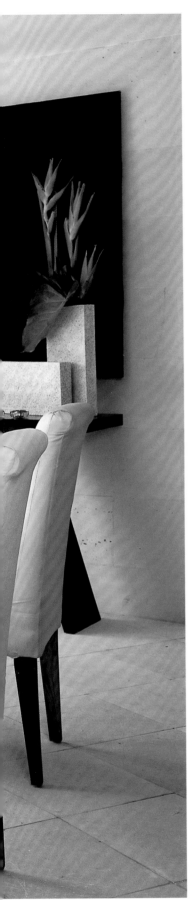

above The elegant composition of Seiki Torige's handmade plates and glasses paired with his rough-hewn recycled vases lends an air of ethereal sophistication to any dining experience. **left** Reinforcing the room's organic theme is this glass-topped table on *paras Kerobokan* stone blocks. The interaction between the exterior and interior spaces is an important design feature of the villa. The teak decking here makes for a seamless transition from the pool to dining area. The black tones of the console and modern painting offer a striking contrast to the delicate glassware.

dignified dining   Simplicity can still convey a sense of grandeur by using big proportions and serious materials, as seen in this dining space created by Abacus Design for the Grande Oriental suite in Sky Villas Bangkok.

above With the sliding doors fully drawn open, the kitchen merges with the dining room. The chef takes center stage at the stove island.

left Formal accessories such as these gold plate liners and fili-gree napkin rings set a dignified tone for formal entertaining at this otherwise simple glass table.

opposite Cove lighting adds a sense of grandeur to the condo space by reflecting the light upward, thus creating the illusion of a higher ceiling.

modern zen   Japanese minimalism enters the kitchen in this condo unit in Sky Villas Bangkok. This zen-look space designed by DWP Cityspace interprets the cooking area as a tranquil place that's soothing enough to meditate in.

left The high-style kitchen counter doubles as glamorous entertaining space to supplement the dining and living rooms beyond.

above The rattan hanging lamps and vase made of water hyacinth fibers show how Thai designers have re-interpreted traditional materials as modern textures.

above right The long, cool bar mimics the feel of a sushi counter, with La Palma stools adding a touch of Italian chic.

eclectic retro Conceived and decorated by owner Rika Dila as a place for friends to gather and relax, the Chi restaurant at the H1 complex in Bangkok is broken into rooms with different themes embodying feminine fun with a funky edge.

right The moniker, Hula Room, comes from the circular motif on the walls and ceiling of this retro-flavored room. The furniture is vintage '50s. A granny-style sofa offers cozy comfort, balanced by vintage chairs. A trail of dainty butterflies ascending to the ceiling adds feminine delicacy to the room's bold colors and shapes. **left** Trimmings triumph in the private dining room, otherwise known as the Granny Room. Cluttered kitsch and vintage Chinese accessories evoke the brick-a-brack charm of a little old granny's study, mixed with mod striped walls and a mirror mosaic to give it a modern edge.

The authors would like to express their thanks to the following people who gave their kind support during the production of this book:

BALI
Jose Luis Calle at The Bale, Antony Liu Budiwihardja, Arthur Chondros at Downtown Apartments, Jaya Ibrahim, Anjarini Kencahyati, Richard North Lewis of Stoneworks, Daniel Ellaway of Nine Squares, Shinta Siregar of Nexus Studio Architects, Hansjorg Meier and Tomoka Yamamoto at The Legian, and Gill Wilson.

Valentina Audrito email: vale-studio65@dps.centrin.net.id

Veronique Aonzo email: mymonamour@ hotmail.com

Antony Liu Budiwihardja Jl Raya Perjuangan, Kompleks Plaza Kebun Jeruk Blok E-11, Jakarta Barat 11530, tel: (62) 021 535 0319/25/34

Espace Concept www.espaceconcept.net

GM Architects email: gmarc@tiscalinet.it

Jaya Ibrahim email: jayaoffice@cbn.net.id

Jenggala Keramik Jln Uluwatu II, Jimbaran Bali, tel: (62) 361 703 311, www.jenggala-bali.com

Modula Interior & Furniture Legian Kaja 470, Kuta Bali, tel/fax: (62) 361 758 293, email: modulain@yahoo.com

Nexus Studio Architects Perkantoran Duta Wijaya, Unit 1, Jl Raya Puputan, Denpasar Bali, tel: (62) 361 744 3493, email: nexus@dps.centrin.net.id

Nine Squares www.ninesquares.com

Pesamuan Jln Pungutan 25, Sanur Bali, www.pesamuan-bali.com

Seiki Torige Galeri Esok Lusa, Jl Raya Basangkasa 47, Seminyak Kuta, 80361, tel/fax: (62) 361 735 262, email: gundul@eksadata.com

MALAYSIA
Lillian Tay of Veritas Architects.

Veritas Architects 148 Jln Ampang, Kuala Lumpur 50450, tel: (03) 2162 2300, www.veritas.com.my

SINGAPORE
Kevin Tan of aKTa-rchitects, Ernesto Bedmar of Bedmar & Shi, Marcel Heijnen of Chemistry Design, Jean Khoo of City Developments, Sim Boon Yang and Calvin Sim of Eco-id Architects, Michael Cu Fua of Cu Fua Associates, Raymond Seow of Free Space Intent, Guz Wilkinson of Guz Wilkinson Architects, Han

Loke Kwang and Hilary Lo of HYLA Architects, Richard Ho of Richard Ho Architects, Angelena Chan of Index Design, Ko Shiou Hee and Romain Destremau of K2LD Architects, Lim Ai Tiong of LATO Design, Yasuhiro Koichi of Design Studio Spin, Geri Archer of Mara Miri, Dr Stanley SH Quek of Region Development, Anthony Ross of Sentosa Resort and Spa and Benny Cheng of space_craft.

aKTa-rchitects 25 Seah Street #05-01, S'pore 188381, tel: (65) 6333 4331, www.akta.com.sg

American Fine Furnishing Gallery #02-26 Raffles Hotel Arcade, 328 North Bridge Rd, S'pore 188719, tel: (65) 6339 2648

Arclinea www.arclinea.it

Barang Barang #01-35 Great World City, S'pore 237994, tel: (65) 6738 0133

Bedmar & Shi 12A Keong Saik Rd, S'pore 089119, tel: (65) 6227 7117, email: bedmar.shi@pacific.net.sg

Chemistry Design www.chemistryteam.com

Club 21 Gallery Four Seasons Hotel, #01-07/8, 190 Orchard Blvd, S'pore 248646, tel: (65) 6887 5451, www.clubtwentyone.com

Colonial Antique 28 Lorong Ampas S'pore 328781, tel: (65) 6254 0595, email: cantique@singnet.com.sg

Cream 136 136 Bukit Timah Rd, S'pore 229838, tel: (65) 6836 3591, email: cream136@pacific.net.sg

Cu Fua Associates 43B Dickson Rd, S'pore 209518, tel: (65) 6291 1172, www.cufua.com

d'apres nous 22 Duxton Hill, S'pore 089605, tel: (65) 6423 0655, www.d-apres-nous.com

De La Espada www.delaespada.com

Design Studio Spin email: spin@msb.biglobe.ne.jp

Eco-id Architects 11 Stamford Rd, #04-06, Capitol Bldg, S'pore 178884, tel: (65) 6337 5119, email: ecoid@pacific.net.sg

Enrique Martinez Celaya www.martinezcelaya.com

Evershine Gallery www.evershinegallery.com

FLOS www.flos.com

Fluv Floral Stylists www.fluv.com.sg

Free Space Intent 80 Nicoll Hwy #01-84, S'pore 188836, tel: (65) 6334 2150, www.freespace.com.sg

Gaggenau www.gaggenau.com

Galerie Cho Lon 43 Jln Merah Saga 01-76, S'pore 278115, tel: (65) 6473 7922, email: info@cho-lon.com

Guz Wilkinson Architects 14B Murray Terrace, S'pore 079525, tel: (65) 6224 2182, www.guzarchitects.com

HYLA Architects 47 Ann Siang Rd #02-01, S'pore 069720, tel: (65) 6324 2488, www.hyla.com.sg

Index Design 15-A Purvis St, S'pore 188594, tel: (65) 6220 1002

K2LD Architects 136 Bukit Timah Rd, S'pore 229838, tel: (65) 6738 7277, www.K2LD.com

kzdesigns tel/fax:(65) 6836 3365, www.kzdesigns.com

Le Klint www.leklint.com

Lifestorey www.lifestorey.com

The Life Shop www.thelifeshop.com

Lightcraft www.lightcraft.com.sg

The Link Boutique #01-10 Palais Renaissance, 390 Orchard Rd, S'pore 238871, tel: (65) 6737 7503, www.TheLink.com.sg

Loop email: loop@go4.it

MARA MIRI email: gnrptltd@singnet.com.sg

Orientation #01-03 Stamford House, 39 Stamford Rd, S'pore 178885, tel: (65) 6338 1125, www.orientation-home.com

Richard Ho Architects 691 East Coast Rd, S'pore 459057, tel: (65) 6446 4811

Sottsass Associati www.sottsass.it

space_craft 324 River Valley Rd, S'pore 238356, tel: (65) 6333 3108, www.spacecraft.com.sg

Space Furniture Millenia Walk Level 2, 9 Raffles Blvd, S'pore 039596

The Touch www.thetouch.com.sg

V. Hive Home Interiors 109, North Bridge Rd, #02-37/41 Funan the IT Mall, S'pore 179097, tel: (65) 6338 9348

Villeroy & Boch www.villeroy-boch.com

X·TRA Living www.xtra.com.sg

THAILAND
Diana Moxon of Anantara Resort & Spa Hua Hin, Rika Dila, Chananun Theeravanvilai of Chime Design,

Benjawan Sudhikam and Daranee Suthivong of the Conrad Bangkok, Arthur Napolitano, Alexander Hutton-Potts, Orbit Design, Carolyn Corogin of C2 Studio, Vichien Chansevikul and Michael Palmer, Andreas and Petcharat Richter, Delia Oakins of Carpediem Galleries, Brian Renaud, H Ernest Lee of H Gallery, Jacques Baume, Sylvain Guisetti of Lotus Lifestyle Gallery, Alex Lamont of Lamont Contemporary, Debbie Thio and Supranee Taecharungroj of The Metropolitan Bangkok, Lalana Lauren Santos of Dusit Hotels and Resorts, Arlada Jumsai na Ayudhya of the Dusit Thani Bangkok, Kessiri Loilawa and Nusra Kongsujarit of Challenge Property, Urs Zimmerman, Pornsak Rattanamethanon of H1, Pornsri Rojmeta of To Die For, Nachanok Ratchanadaros of Extase, Kittima Kritiyachotipakorn and Kingkaew Puengjesada of Golden Land Property Development and Laura Herne of Outlaurs.

Abacus Design 144 (off) Soi Siripot, Sukhumvit 81, Bangkok 10250, tel: (662) 742 4571 6/331 9966

Anyroom 4th Floor Siam Discovery Center, Bangkok 10330, tel: (662) 658 0583, www.anyroom.com

C2 Studio The Prime Bldg, Level 15, Suites B&C, 24 Sukhumvit 21, Bangkok 10110, tel: (662) 260 4243, email: Carolyn@c2studio.net

Carpediem Galleries #1B-1 Ruam Rudee Bldg, 566 Ploenchit Rd, Bangkok 10330, tel: (662) 250 0408, email: deliaok@loxinfo.co.th

DWP Cityspace www.dwpartnership.com

H Gallery 201 Sathorn Soi 12, Bangkok 10500, tel: (661) 310 4428, email: ernest3@hotmail.com

Habitat Bangkok www.habitat.net

IAW Soi Panich-Anan Sukhumvit 71, Bangkok 10110, tel: (662) 713 1237, email: iawbkk@loxinfo.co.th

Lamont Contemporary 3/F Shop 23, Gaysorn Plaza, 999 Ploenchit Rd, Bangkok 10330, tel: (662) 656 1250, email: lamont@lamont-design.com

Orbit Design Unit 2A, 2nd Floor, M Thai Tower, All Seasons Place, 87 Wireless Rd, Bangkok 10330, tel: (662) 654 3667, www.orbitdesignstudio.com

Sky Villas The Ascott Bangkok, 187 South Sathorn Rd, Bangkok 10120, tel: (662) 676 8888, www.goldenlandplc.com

State Tower www.challenge.co.th

Vihayas www.vihayas.co.th